SPANISH FOR REAL

LA CUCARACHA SARA

Copyright © 2024 by La Cucaracha Sara Inc. All rights reserved. No part of this book may be reproduced, distributed, or transmitted in any form or by any means, without the prior written permission of the publisher, except in the case of brief quotations embodied in critical reviews and certain other noncommercial uses permitted by copyright law.
Names, characters, places, and incidents are products of the author's imagination or are used fictitiously.

Printed in the United States of America.

First Edition 2024

ISBN: 979-8-9894433-2-1 (print)

Introduction

Learn Spanish That Actually Matters!

Get ready to explore a fresh approach to learning!
So often, traditional resources give you lessons that are simply out of touch with everyday conversations.
Let's go beyond the basics and discover how to truly communicate like a native!

> ¡Hola! Yo soy
> La Cucaracha Sara
> and I teach Mexican slang.

¡BIENVENIDOS DE VUELTA!

FOLLOW ME

◉ @la.cucaracha.sara

♪ @la.cucaracha.sara

▶ @la.cucaracha.sara

ⓟ @lacucarachasara

🌐 www.glotmour.com

TABLE OF CONTENTS

Lesson 1   Grammar

Lesson 2   Everyday Spanish

Lesson 3   Mexican Slang

Lesson 4   Love

Lesson 5   Wellbeing

Lesson 6   Home and Family

Lesson 7   GRWM

Lesson 8   Shopping

GRAMMAR

NOTES:

NOTES:

Grammar

Ser vs. Estar

Both verbs mean 'to be' but are used differently.

Ser ⟶ Soy: used for permanent states, characteristics, origin, time.
- Soy de Chicago – I am from Chicago.

Estar ⟶ Estoy: used for temporary states, location, emotions.
- Estoy aburrido – I am bored.

Gender of Nouns

Most nouns in Spanish are either masculine or feminine.

Masculine nouns usually end in –o.
Feminine nouns usually end in –a.
There are exceptions, such as el día (the day) and la mano (the hand). In Book 1: Spanish in 60 Days, you will find more examples of masculine and feminine nouns, along with their exceptions.

Subject Pronouns Are Often Omitted.

In Spanish, the subject pronoun (yo, tú, él/ella – I, you, he/she) is often omitted because the verb conjugation indicates the subject. For example, hablo means "I speak," so yo is unnecessary unless you want to emphasize the subject.

Verb Conjugation

Verbs change according to tense (when the action happens) and subject (who is performing the action).

Subject Pronoun	Verb in Present Tense	Verbs in the Past Tense
Yo (I)	hablo (I speak)	hablé (I spoke)
Tú (you)	hablas (you speak)	hablaste (you spoke)
Él/Ella	habla (He/She speaks)	habló (He/She spoke)

Noun–Adjective Agreement

In Spanish, adjectives need to match the gender (masculine or feminine) and number (singular or plural) of the noun they describe.

Definite Articles (equivalent to "the" in English)

Gender	Singular	Plural
masculine	el	los
feminine	la	las

Masculine Singular ⟶ <u>El</u> perro negro. - The black dog.
Masculine Plural ⟶ <u>Los</u> perros negros. - The black dogs.

Feminine Singular ⟶ <u>La</u> casa grande. - The big house.
Feminine Plural ⟶ <u>Las</u> casas grandes. - The big houses.

Indefinite Articles (equivalent to "a/an" or "some" in English)

Gender	Singular	Plural
masculine	un	unos
feminine	una	unas

Masculine Singular ⟶ <u>Un</u> perro. - A dog.
Masculine Plural ⟶ <u>Unos</u> perros. - Some dogs.

Feminine Singular ⟶ <u>Una</u> flor. - A flower.
Feminine Plural ⟶ <u>Unas</u> flores. - Some flowers.

Reflexive verbs in Spanish indicate that the subject both performs and receives the action of the verb. These verbs are accompanied by reflexive pronouns, which reflect the person and number of the subject.

Reflexive Pronouns

me	→	myself, I
te	→	yourself
se	→	himself/herself/itself (for singular third person)
nos	→	ourselves
se	→	themselves/yourselves (for plural third person)

Acostarse is a reflexive verb that means 'to lie down' or 'to go to bed.' Because *acostarse* is a reflexive verb, it requires a reflexive pronoun that matches the subject.

<u>Me acuesto</u> a las 10 de la noche.	I go to bed at 10 PM.
<u>Te acuestas</u> temprano.	You go to bed early.
<u>Se acuesta</u> temprano.	He/She goes to bed early.
<u>Nos acostamos</u> en el pasto.	We lie down on the grass.
<u>Se</u> acuestan en la cama.	They lie down in the bed.

Bañarse is a reflexive verb that means 'to bathe oneself' or 'to shower'.

Me <u>baño</u> todos los días. – I <u>shower</u> every day.

- *Baño* is the verb *bañarse* conjugated in the first person singular.
- *Me* is the reflexive pronoun for 'I.'

How to Form Reflexive Verbs

Reflexive verbs in Spanish have *–se* at the end of their infinitive form.

- Remove the *–se* from the verb.
- Conjugate the verb normally based on the subject.
- Place the reflexive pronoun before the verb or attach it to the infinitive.

Conjugation of *bañarse* in Present Tense

Yo me baño	I shower
Tú te bañas	You bathe yourself (informal)
Él/Ella/Usted se baña	He/She/You (formal) bathes
Nosotros(as) nos bañamos	We bathe ourselves
Ellos/Ellas/Ustedes se bañan	They/You all bathe themselves

As a reflexive verb, *bañarse* always requires a reflexive pronoun that agrees with the subject of the sentence.

Here are some common reflexive verbs in Spanish:

Vestirse – to get dressed
- <u>Me visto</u> rápidamente. – I get dressed quickly.

Sentarse – to sit down
- <u>Nos sentamos</u> juntos. – We sit together.

Peinarse – to comb one's hair
- <u>Me peino</u> cada mañana. – I comb my hair every morning.

Levantarse – to get up
- <u>Me levanto</u> a las ocho. – I get up at 8.

Lavarse – to wash oneself
- <u>Se lava</u> las manos. – He/she washes his/her hands.

> **Reflexive verbs play a key role in Spanish, especially when referring to self-care, routines, and daily activities.**

Indirect Object Pronouns

Indirect object pronouns indicate to whom or for whom an action is done. They are used with verbs to show who receives the benefit of the action.

me	⟶	to me
te	⟶	to you
le	⟶	to him/her/*you(formal)*
nos	⟶	to us
les	⟶	to them/*you all(formal)*

<u>Le doy</u> un regalo a Luisa. – I give a gift to Luisa.

Here, 'le' is the indirect object pronoun that tells us to whom the gift is given.

> **In most cases, the indirect object pronoun is placed directly before the conjugated verb in the sentence.**

The verb *gustar* can be confusing for English speakers because it operates differently from the English verb "to like."

In Spanish, *gustar* means "to be pleasing to." This means that in a sentence, what is liked is the subject, not the person who likes it. So, when you talk about what someone likes, you express what is pleasing to them.

Me gusta el libro. – I like the book.
- Me (refering to myself) is the pronoun.
- Gusta is used because el libro (the book) is singular.

A typical sentence with *gustar* follows this order:

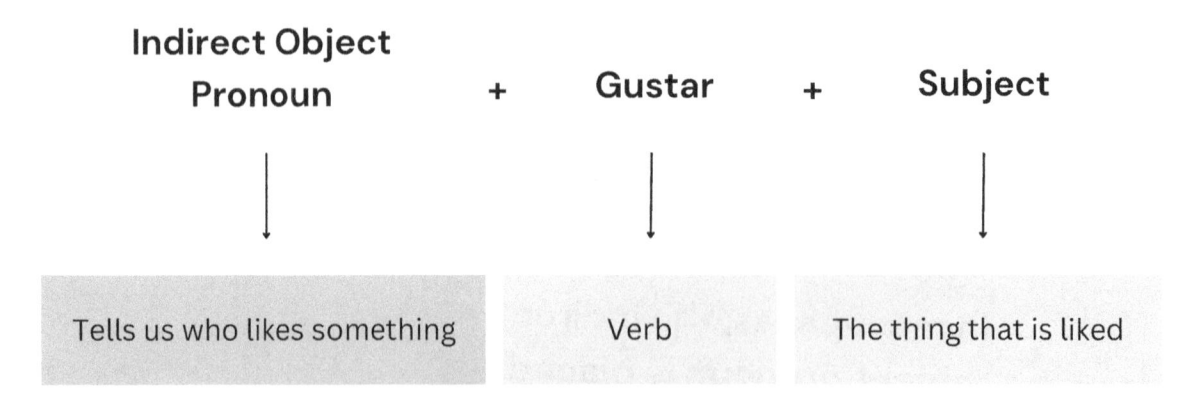

Indirect Object Pronoun	+	Gustar	+	Subject
Tells us who likes something		Verb		The thing that is liked

Use *gusta* when the thing liked is singular.

    Me gusta el helado. – I like ice cream.

Use *gustan* when the thing liked is plural.

    Me gustan las galletas. – I like cookies.

Here are the pronouns you use with *gustar*:
- Me – to me
- Te – to you(informal)
- Le – to him/her/*you(formal)*
- Nos – to us
- Les – to them

Here are some examples with different subjects.

<u>Me gusta</u> la música. – I like music.

   Subject ⟶ la música (music) ⟶ Singular

<u>Te gusta</u> la flor. – You like the flower.

   Subject ⟶ la flor (the flower) ⟶ Singular

<u>Nos gustan</u> los libros. – We like books.

   Subject ⟶ los libros (the books) ⟶ Plural

<u>Les gustan</u> las películas. – They like the movies.

   Subject ⟶ las películas (the movies) ⟶ Plural

Common Abbreviations & Acronyms

EEUU	**Estados Unidos** (es-ta-dos oo-nee-dos)	United States
Sr.	**Señor** (seh-nyohr)	Sir
Sra.	**Señora** (seh-nyoh-rah)	Mrs.
Srta.	**Señorita** (seh-nyoh-ree-tah)	Ms.
Atte.	**Atentamente** (ah-ten-ta-men-teh)	Sincerely
Profe	**Profesor/Profesora** (pro-feh-sor/pro-feh-sor-ah)	Profesor
GPI	**Gracias por invitar** (gra-see-as por een-vee-tar)	Thanks for the invite
Vdd	**Verdad** (ver-dahd)	True/Truth
Cdt	**Cuídate** (coo-ee-da-teh)	Take care
Pq/Xk	**Porque, por qué** (por-khe, por khe)	Because, Why
Xfa	**Por favor** (por fa-vohr)	Please
Grax	**Gracias** (grah-see-as)	Thanks
X	**Por** (por)	For
D	**De** (deh)	From

Common Abbreviations & Acronyms

Q/K	**Qué** (khe)	What
Ud.	**Usted** (oos-ted)	You (formal)
TQM	**Te quiero mucho** (teh kee-eh-roh moo-cho)	I love you (ILY)
Ntp	**No te preocupes** (noh teh preh-oh-coo-pes)	Don't worry
Ntc	**No te creas** (noh teh creh-ahs)	Just kidding (JK)
QEPD	**Que en paz descanse** (khe en pahz des-cahn-seh)	Rest in Peace (RIP)
Npw	**No pues wow** (no poo-es wow)	Dang that's crazy
Tmbn	**También** (tahm-bee-ehn)	Also, me too
ALV	**A la verga** (ah la ver-gah)	Oh fuck, to hell
BB	**Bebé** (beh-beh)	Baby/babe

Hey! What does PTM mean?

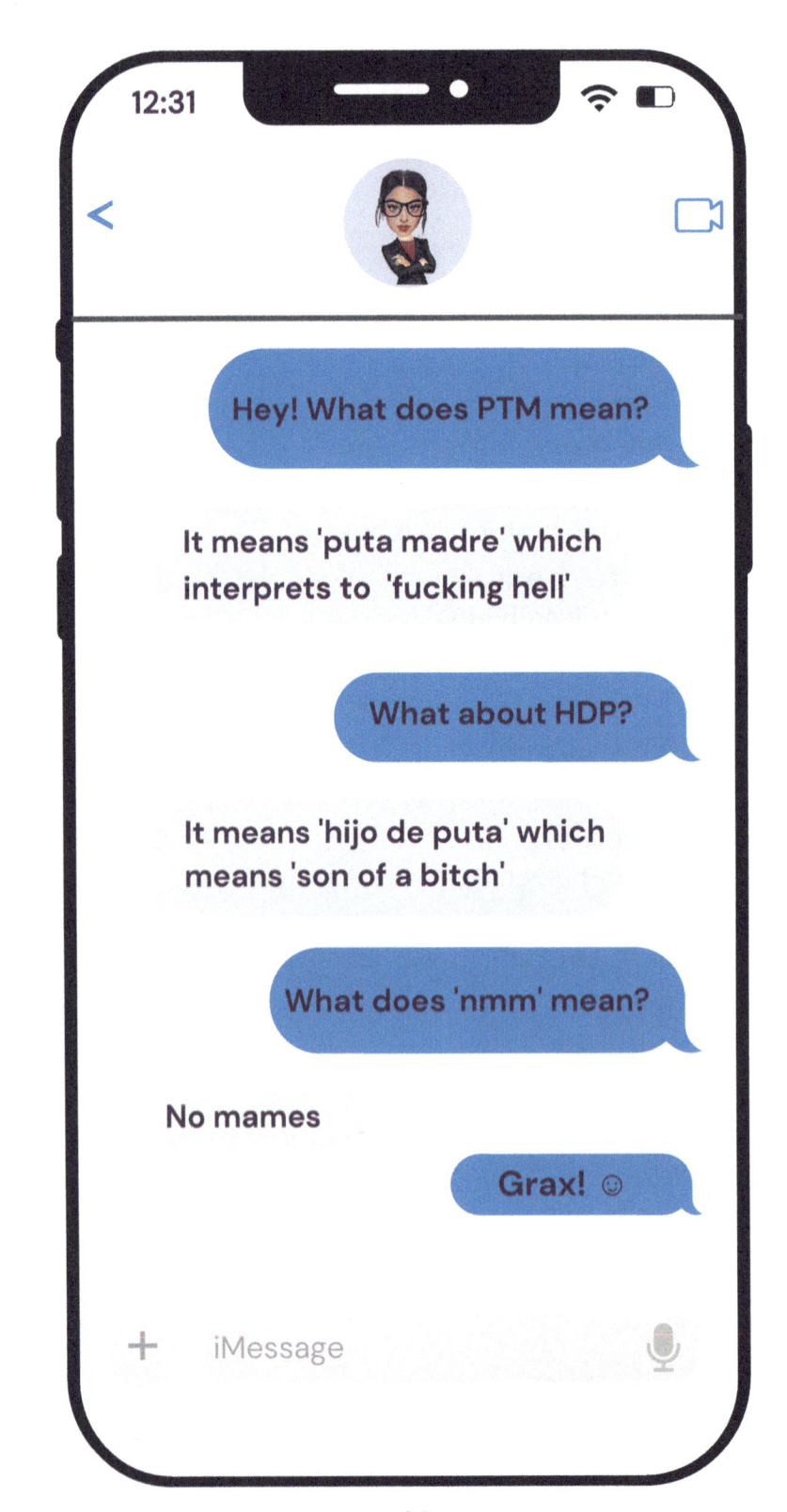

It means 'puta madre' which interprets to 'fucking hell'

What about HDP?

It means 'hijo de puta' which means 'son of a bitch'

What does 'nmm' mean?

No mames

Grax! ☺

TEST YOUR UNDERSTANDING
Lesson 1 Grammar

1. Choose the correct form of the verb 'soy'.

   A. Soy maestra.

   B. Soy en la escuela.

   C. Soy estudiando.

2. What does 'vestirse' mean?

   A. To get up.

   B. To sit down.

   C. To get dressed.

3. Le voy a preparar un cafe. Who is 'le' referring to?

   A. To me.

   B. To him/her.

   C. To them.

4. What is the Spanish abbreviation for 'I Love You'?

   A. ALV

   B. TQM

   C. NTP

EVERYDAY SPANISH

NOTES:

NOTES:

Phrases to Uplift the Room

Todo va a estar bien.
(toh-doh va ah es-tar bee-ehn)

Everything will be okay.

El tiempo lo cura todo.
(el tee-em-poh lo coo-rah toh-doh)

Time heals everything.

No hay mal que por bien no venga.
(no ah-ee mal khe por bee-ehn no ven-gah)

Every cloud has a silver lining.

¡Ánimo!
(ah-nee-moh)

Cheer up!

No pasa nada.
(no pa-sah na-dah)

Nothing's happening/No worries.

Phrases for when Things Feel Off

Tengo un presentimiento sobre esto.
(ten-goh oon preh-sen-tee-mee-en-to so-breh es-toh)

I have a gut feeling about this.

Me da una mala espina.
(meh da oo-nah ma-la es-pee-nah)

I'm sensing bad vibes.

Las apariencias engañan.
(las ah-pa-ree-en-see-as en-ga-nyahn)

Looks can be deceiving.

Me rajé/Me eché para atrás.
(meh ra-heh/meh eh-cheh pa-rah ah-tras)

I got cold feet.

El que se duerme, pierde.
(el khe se doo-er-me pee-er-deh)

You snooze, you lose.

Phrases of Wisdom

Más vale solo/sola que mal acompañado/acompañada.
(mas va-leh so-lo/so-la khe mal ah-com-pa-nyah-doh/ah-com-pah-nyah-dah)

Rather be alone than in bad company.

El que sabe, sabe.
(el khe sa-beh, sa-beh)

If you know, you know.

Más vale tarde que nunca.
(mas va-leh tar-deh khe noon-cah)

Better late than never.

El que quiere, puede.
(el khe kee-eh-reh, poo-eh-deh)

He who wants, will.

Ojo por ojo.
(oh-hoh por oh-hoh)

An eye for an eye.

Phrases to be More Assertive

Prefiero que hagamos esto de otra manera.
(preh-fee-eh-roh khe ah-ga-mos es-toh de oh-tra ma-ne-rah)

I prefer we do this differently.

Me gustaría que respetaras mi opinión.
(meh goos-ta-ree-ah khe res-pe-ta-rahs mee oh-pee-nee-ohn)

I would like you to respect my opinion.

Ya no puedo más.
(yah no poo-eh-doh mas)

I can't take it/do it anymore.

Voy a ser claro/clara.
(voy ah ser cla-roh/cla-rah)

I am going to be clear.

Este es mi punto de vista.
(es-teh es mee poon-toh de vees-tah)

This is my point of view.

Everyday Conversations

¿Qué onda, wey. Qué haces?
(khe on-da whey. khe ah-ses)
What's up, bro/dude. What are you doing?

Nada, ¿y tú?
(nah-da, ee too)
Nothing, and you?

Estoy trabajando.
(es-toy tra-ba-han-doh)
I am working.

Voy de camino a la tienda.
(voy deh ca-mee-noh ah la tee-en-dah)
I'm on my way to the store.

Everyday Conversations

Do you want to go out tonight?

O sea, sí, pero no. Tengo que trabajar mañana.
(oh seh-ah see, pe-roh noh. Ten-go khe tra-ba-har ma-nyah-nah)
I mean, yes, but no. I have to work tomorrow.

¿Cómo estuvo tu viaje a México?
(co-mo es-too-vo too vee-ah-heh ah Meh-hee-coh)

How was your trip to Mexico?

¡Estuvo a todo dar!
(es-too-vo ah toh-doh dahr)
It's was great!

Different Ways to Say A LOT, TOO MUCH

mucho - a lot
(moo-choh)
↳ Tengo <u>mucho</u> trabajo esta semana. - I have <u>a lot</u> of work this week.

muchísimo/muchísima - an awful lot
(moo-chee-see-moh/moo-chee-see-mah)
↳ Había <u>muchísima</u> gente en el concierto. - There were <u>an awful lot</u> of people at the concert.

demasiado - too much, too many
(deh-ma-see-ah-doh)
↳ Trabajas <u>demasiado</u>. - You work <u>too much</u>.

un montón - a lot
(oon mohn-tohn)
↳ Me divertí <u>un montón</u>. - I had <u>a lot</u> of fun.

harto/harta - plenty
(ahr-toh) (ahr-tah)
↳ Hay <u>harta</u> comida en el refri. - There's <u>plenty</u> of food in the fridge.

un chingo - too fucking much
(oon cheen-goh)
↳ Te quiero <u>un chingo</u>. - I love you <u>so fucking much</u>.

un chorro - a shit-ton
(oon cho-rroh)
↳ Tengo <u>un chorro</u> de cosas que hacer. - I have <u>a shit-ton</u> of things to do.

un chingomadral - a fuck-ton, a lot
(oon cheen-go-ma-dral)
↳ Hay un <u>chingomadral</u> de tráfico hoy. - There is a <u>fuck-ton</u> of traffic today.

Different Ways to Say GREAT, AMAZING

genial - great
(heh-nee-al)
↳ Te ves <u>genial</u> en ese vestido. - You look <u>great</u> in that dress.

chido/chida - cool, great
(chee-doh/chee-dah)
↳ Esa canción está muy <u>chida</u>. - That song is so <u>cool</u>.

padre - cool, amazing
(pah-dreh)
↳ La película estuvo <u>padre</u>. - The movie was <u>amazing</u>.

de pelos - great, amazing
(deh pe-los)
↳ Me la pasé <u>de pelos.</u> - I had a <u>great</u> time.

chingón - fucking badass, really great
(cheen-gohn)
↳ El nuevo álbum de la banda está bien <u>chingón</u>. - The band's new album is really <u>fucking great</u>.

a toda madre - really great
(ah toh-dah ma-dreh)
↳ El concierto estuvo <u>a toda madre</u>. - The concert was <u>really great</u>.

perron/perrona - cool, awesome
(peh-rron/peh-rron-ah)
↳ Tu moto está <u>perrona</u>. - Your motorcycle is <u>awesome</u>.

Different Ways to Say CHILD

niño/niña - boy/girl, child
(nee-nyoh/nee-nyah)
↳ El <u>niño</u> esta llorando. - The <u>boy</u> is crying.

mijo/mija - my son/daughter or honey, dear
(mee-hoh/mee-hah)
↳ Gracias <u>mija</u>, eres muy tierna. - Thanks <u>dear</u>, you're so sweet.

chamaco/chamaca - kid
(chah-ma-coh/chah-ma-cah)
↳ Oye, <u>chamaco</u>. ¿Quieres un helado? - Hey, <u>kid</u>. Do you want an ice cream?

mocoso/mocosa - snotty/bratty child *this word has a negative connotation*
(mo-co-soh/mo-co-sah)
↳ El <u>mocoso</u> de mi sobrino arruinó mi maquillage. - My <u>bratty</u> nephew ruined my makeup.

escuincle/escuincla - kid *this word has a negative connotation*
(es-kwin-cleh/es-kwin-cla)
↳ Esos <u>escuincles</u> se andan peleando. - Those <u>kids</u> are fighting.

chiquillo/chiquilla - boy/girl
(chee-kee-yo/chee-kee-ya)
↳ Ese <u>chiquillo</u> sabe bailar. - That <u>boy</u> knows how to dance.

pequeño/pequeña - little guy/little girl
(pe-ke-nyoh/pe-ke-nyah)
↳ El papá juega con su <u>pequeña</u>. - The dad plays with his <u>little girl</u>.

Different Ways to Say HOME

casa - home/house
(kah-sah)

↳ Mi casa tiene un jardín hermoso. - My house has a beautiful garden.

domicilio - residence/address
(doh-mee-see-lee-oh)

↳ Envia el paquete a mi domicilio. - Send the package to my address.

residencia - residence
(reh-see-dhen-see-ah)

↳ Mi residencia está cerca de la universidad. - My residence is near the university.

hogar - home/household
(oh-ghar)

↳ Después de un largo viaje, no hay nada mejor que volver al hogar. - After a long trip, there's nothing better than coming back home.

cantón - house/home, someones place
(kahn-tohn)

↳ Pásale a mi cantón cuando quieras. - Come over to my place whenever you want.

Different Ways to Say SAD

apenado/apenada - sorrow
(ah-pe-na-doh/ah-pe-na-dah)

↳ Estoy <u>apenada</u> por la pérdida de tu gato. - I'm <u>saddened</u> by the loss of your cat.

bajoneado/bajoneada - feeling down/bummed out
(ba-hoh-ne-ah-doh/ba-hoh-ne-ah-dah)

↳ Amanecí un poco <u>bajoneada</u>. - I woke up <u>feeling</u> a bit <u>down</u>.

melancólico/melancólica - melancholic
(meh-lan-co-lee-coh/meh-lan-co-lee-cah)

↳ La despedida me dejó <u>melancólico</u>. - The farewell left me <u>melancholic</u>.

desanimado/desanimada - discouraged
(des-ah-nee-ma-doh/des-ah-nee-ma-dah)

↳ El equipo estaba <u>desanimado</u> tras la derrota. - The team was <u>discouraged</u> after the defeat.

agüitado/agüitada - gloomy
(ah-goo-ee-ta-doh/ah-goo-ee-ta-dah)

↳ ¿Por qué tan <u>agüitada</u>? - Why so <u>gloomy</u>?

deprimido/deprimida - depressed
(de-pree-mee-doh/de-pree-mee-dah)

↳ Me siento <u>deprimida</u> porque extraño a mi familia. - I feel <u>depressed</u> because I miss my family.

triste - sad
(trees-teh)

↳ Esa canción está muy <u>triste</u>. - That song is very <u>sad</u>.

MEXICAN SLANG

NOTES:

NOTES:

Mexican Slang

hijole – holy cow, oh my gosh
(ee-ho-leh)

↳ This expression can convey excitement or disbelief depending on the context.

ah, jijo – wow, oh snap
(ah hee-ho)

↳ This expression is a more informal variation of "hijole".

carajo – hell, damn, dammit
(ca-rah-ho)

↳ ¿Qué carajos dices? - What the hell are you saying?

al tiempo – room temperature
(ahl tee-em-poh)

↳ ¿Me das una agua al tiempo? - Can I have a room temperature water?

poner los cuernos – infidelity, cheating on you significant other
(po-ner los coo-ehr-nos)

↳ Me pusieron los cuernos - I got cheated on
   Le puse los cuernos - I cheated on him/her
   Le pusieron los cuernos - he/she got cheated on

¿A poco? – Really? Is that so?
(ah po-coh)

> Me pusieron los cuernos otra vez.

> I got cheated on again.

> ¿A poco? ¡Qué pendejo/a!

> Really? What a dumbass!

Mexican Slang

eso que ni qué – no doubt about it, ain't that the truth
(eh-so khe nee khe)

↳ Mi compañera de trabajo es muy bonita, <u>eso que ni qué</u>, pero tiene una actitud muy desagradable. - My coworker is very pretty, <u>no doubt about it</u>, but she has a very unpleasant attitude.

ándale – hurry up, come on, alright
(ahn-da-leh)

↳ ¡<u>Ándale</u>, que ya es tarde! - <u>Hurry up</u>, it's already late!

¡<u>Ándale</u>, acompáñame! - <u>Come on</u>, go with me!

¡<u>Ándale</u>, pues! Te veo al rato. - <u>Alright</u> then, I'll see you in a bit.

banda – crew, group of friends
(bahn-dah)

↳ Invité a toda la <u>banda</u> a la carne asada. - I invited the whole <u>crew</u> to the BBQ

apantallar – to impress, show off
(ah-pan-tah-yar)

↳ Él quería <u>apantallar</u> a sus amigos. - He wanted to <u>show off</u> to his friends.

Mi novia realmente <u>apantalló</u> a mi familia con su habilidad para cocinar. - My girlfriend really <u>impressed</u> my family with her cooking skills.

andar con todo – going all out, high level enthusiasm
(ahn-dar khon toh-doh)

↳ Él/Ella <u>anda con todo</u>. - He/She is <u>going all out</u>.

(Yo) <u>ando con todo.</u> - I am <u>going all out</u>.

Mexican Slang

bronca – conflict, a fight
(brohn-cah)

↳ Siempre que salimos, acabamos en una <u>bronca</u>.   -   Every time we go out, we end up in a <u>fight</u>.

relajo – ruckus, chaos
(reh-la-hoh)

↳ Mi mejor amiga y yo somos un pinche <u>relajo</u>.   -   My bestie and I are a fucking <u>chaos</u>.

hacerla de tos – to cause a scene, cause a fuss
(ah-ser-lah deh tos)

↳ No la <u>hagas de tos</u>.   -   Don't <u>make a scene</u>.

   La <u>hizo de tos.</u>   -   He/she <u>made a scene</u>.

   La <u>hicieron de tos</u>.   -   They <u>made a fuss</u>.

estar en la ruina – broke, struggling financially
(es-tahr en lah roo-ee-nah)

↳ Quedé <u>en la ruina</u> después de pagar mis deudas.   -   I'm <u>broke</u> after paying off my debts.

hacer pendejadas – doing dumdass/stupid things
(ah-ser pen-de-ha-das)

↳ No <u>hagas pendejadas.</u>   -   Don't <u>do stupid things</u>.

   Haces muchas <u>pendejadas</u>.   -   You do a lot of <u>stupid things</u>.

Mexican Slang

jetón/jetóna – asleep, knocked out
(heh-tohn/heh-toh-nah)

> ¿Saliste anoche?

> No, me quede bien <u>jetón.</u>

> Did you go out last night?

> No, <u>I knocked out</u> / I <u>fell asleep</u>.

jeta – a vulgar way to say face/mouth
(heh-tah)

↳ ¡Cierra la <u>jeta</u>!   -   Shut your <u>mouth</u>!

cañón – rough, an intense situation
(cah-nyohn)

↳ Está <u>cañón</u> con este calor.   -   It's <u>really rough</u> with this heat.

chicloso/chiclosa – person who's too attached, clingy
(chee-clo-soh/chee-clo-sah)

↳ No estes de <u>chiclosa</u>, deja que tu novio respire.   -   Don't be <u>clingy</u>, let your boyfriend breathe.

chiqueado/chiqueada – spoiled, pampered
(chee-kee-ah-doh/chee-kee-ah-dah)

↳ Mi novia está muy <u>chiqueada</u> gracias a mí.   -   My girlfriend is very <u>spoiled</u> thanks to me.

Mexican Slang

largarse – to leave, to go away *this word has a harsh forceful tone*
(lar-gar-seh)

↳ Lárgate de aquí. - Get out of here.
 ¿Por qué no te largas de una vez? - Why don't you just leave already?

pasarse de lanza – overstepping boundaries, crossing the line
(pa-sar-se de lan-zah)

↳ No te pases de lanza conmigo. - Don't cross the line with me.

meter la pata – to make a mistake, to mess up
(meh-ter la pa-tah)

↳ Metí la pata y empeoré la situación. - I messed up and made the situation worse.

estar en las nubes – daydreaming, distracted
(es-tar en las noo-bes)

↳ No escuchaste lo que dije porque estabas en las nubes. - You didn't hear what I said because you were daydreaming.

echar un vistazo – take a look, glance
(eh-char oon veez-tah-zoh)

↳ Echale un vistazo al menú y dime qué te apetece. - Take a look at the menu and tell me what you'd like.

Mexican Slang

fregar – vulgar way to say annoy, irritate, bother
(freh-gar)

↳ No me vengas a fregar. - Don't come and bother me.

qué flojera – lack of motivation, what a drag
(khe flo-her-ah)

↳ Otra reunión en el trabajo que durará horas… ¡qué flojera! - Another work meeting that will last for hours… what a drag!

chambeador/chambeadora – hard worker
(cham-beh-ah-dohr/cham-beh-ah-dora)

↳ Mi papá es un chambeador. - My dad is a hard worker.

alivianado/alivianada – a chill, laidback person
(ah-lee-vee-ah-na-doh/ah-lee-vee-ah-na-dah)

↳ Aunque tenemos mucho trabajo, mi jefe es bastante alivianado y no nos presiona. - Even though we have a lot of work, my boss is quite chill and doesn't pressure us.

aplácate – calm down, settle down
(ah-pla-ca-teh)

↳ ¡Aplácate! No es para tanto. - Calm down! It's not a big deal.

Mexican Slang

enchilado/enchilada – the burning sensation of eating something spicy or being mad
(en-chee-la-doe/en-chee-la-dah)

↳ Estoy <u>enchilado</u> con estas alas de pollo. - I am <u>feeling the heat</u> from these wings.

Mi amigo se <u>enchiló</u> cuando no le puse atención. - My friend <u>got pissed</u> when I didn't pay attention to him.

aventarse – taking a risk, going for something
(ah-ven-tar-seh)

↳ (yo) Me <u>aventé</u>. - I <u>went for it</u>.
(el/ella) Se <u>aventó</u>. - He/she <u>took a risk.</u>

hacer la lucha – to make an effort
(ah-ser la loo-cha)

↳ Voy a <u>hacer la lucha</u>. - I am going <u>to make an effort</u>.
Él/ella <u>hizo la lucha</u>. - He/she <u>made an effort</u>.

tirar la toalla – 'throw in the towel', to give up
(tee-rahr la toe-ah-yah)

↳ El equipo estaba perdiendo por una gran diferencia y el entrenador decidió <u>tirar la toalla.</u> - The team was losing by a large margin, and the coach decided to <u>throw in the towel.</u>

Mexican Slang

bola de culeros/culeras – a bunch of assholes
(boh-lah de coo-ler-ohs/coo-ler-ahs)

bola de pendejos/pendejas – a bunch of dumbasses/idiots
(boh-lah de pen-de-hos/pen-de-hahs)

culo – ass
(koo-loh)

pinche culero – fucking asshole
(peen-che coo-leh-roh)

Fregadazo, putazo, & una chinga = a fucking beating.

Informal	Formal	Meaning
Me caí y me di un <u>fregadazo</u>. (meh ca-ee ee meh dee oon fre-ga-da-soh)	**Me caí y <u>me pegué fuerte</u>.** (meh ca-ee ee meh pe-geh foo-ehr-te)	I fell and took <u>a hard hit</u>.
Hubo <u>putazos</u> anoche. (oo-boh poo-ta-zos ah-no-che)	**Hubo una <u>pelea</u> anoche.** (oo-boh oo-nah pe-le-ah ah-no-che)	There was a <u>fight</u> last night.
Les pusieron <u>una chinga</u>. (les poo-see-eh-rohn oo-na cheen-gah)	**Los <u>golpearon</u>.** (los gol-peh-ah-rohn)	They got <u>beat up</u>.

LOVE

NOTES:

NOTES:

Terms of Endearment
palabras de cariño

mi amor — my love
(mee ah-mohr)

mi amorcito — my little love
(mee ah-mohr-see-toh)

mi consentido/consentida — my pampered sweetie
(mee kohn-sen-tee-doh/kohn-sen-tee-dah)

mi corazón — my heart/my love
(mee koh-ra-zon)

mi corazoncito — my little heart/my little love
(mee koh-ra-zon-see-toh)

mi cielo — my heaven/my sky
(mee see-eh-loh)

mi vida — my life
(mee vee-dah)

mi tesoro — my treasure
(mee tes-oh-roh)

mi luz — my light
(mee looz)

mi alma gemela — my soulmate
(mee al-mah heh-meh-lah)

cariño — darling/sweetheart
(kah-ree-nyoh)

querido/querida — dear
(keh-ree-doh/keh-ree-dah)

Terms of Endearment
palabras de cariño

hermoso/hermosa
(ehr-moh-soh/ehr-moh-sah)

beautiful

precioso/preciosa
(preh-see-oh-soh/preh-see-oh-sah)

precious

chulo/chula
(choo-loh/choo-lah)

good looking

cosita linda
(koh-see-tah leen-dah)

pretty little thing

nena/nene
(neh-nah/neh-neh)

babe

bebé
(beh-beh)

baby

mi rey
(mee reh-ee)

my king

mi reina
(mee reh-ee-nah)

my queen

muñeca/muñeco
(moo-nyeh-cah/moo-nyeh-coh)

doll

muñequito/muñequita
(moo-nyeh-key-toh/moo-nyeh-key-tah)

babydoll

mamita
(mah-mee-tah)

lil mama, mommy

papito
(pah-pee-toh)

daddy

Remember, some terms of endearment in Spanish are appropiate to use with a child, friend, or significant other.

Flirting

Todavía recuerdo el primer día que hablé contigo.
(toh-da-vee-ah re-coo-ehr-doh el pree-mehr dee-ah khe ah-bleh kohn-tee-go)

I still remember the first day I talked to you.

Desde que te conocí, me enamoré de ti.
(des-deh khe teh coh-no-see, meh eh-na-moh-rhe deh tee)

Since I met you, I fell in love with you.

Encantado/encantada de verte.
(en-can-ta-doh/en-can-ta-dah deh ver-teh)

Lovely to see you.

Me gustas mucho.
(meh goos-tas moo-choh)

I like you a lot.

Me gustaría conocerte más.
(meh goos-ta-ree-ah co-no-ser-teh mas)

I would like to get to know you more.

Flirting

Me gusta hablar contigo.
(meh goos-tah ah-blar kohn-tee-go)

I like talking to you.

Quédate conmigo.
(keh-da-teh kohn-mee-goh)

Stay with me.

Te extraño, quiero verte pronto.
(teh ex-tra-nyoh, kee-eh-roh ver-teh pron-toh)

I miss you, I want to see you soon.

Quiero estar contigo.
(kee-eh-roh es-tar kohn-tee-goh)

I want to be with you.

Te vi y me pareciste muy guapo/guapa.
(teh vee ee meh pa-rhe-sis-teh moo-ee goo-ah-poh/goo-ah-pah)

I saw you and thought you were very handsome/beautiful.

Showing Interest in Someone

¿Te puedo llamar?
(teh poo-eh-doh ya-mar)

Can I call you?

Escríbeme
(es-cree-beh-meh)

Text me/Write me.

Espero que sigamos en contacto.
(es-peh-roh khe see-gah-mos en con-tac-toh)

I hope we stay in contact.

Mándame un mensaje cuando puedas.
(mahn-da-meh oon men-sa-heh coo-an-doh poo-eh-das)

Text me when you can.

Ven aquí, mi amor.
(ven ah-kee mee ah-mohr)

Come here, my love.

Approaching Someone

Estoy soltero/soltera.
(es-toy sol-teh-roh/sol-teh-rah)

I'm single.

¿Estás soltero/soltera?
(es-tas sol-teh-roh/sol-teh-rah)

Are you single?

Te presento a mi amigo/amiga.
(teh preh-sen-toh ah mee ah-mee-goh/ah-mee-gah)

Let me introduce you to my friend.

Esta es mi amiga, Maria.
(es-tah es mee ah-mee-gah mah-ree-ah)

This is my friend, Maria.

Le gustas a mi amiga/amigo.
(le goos-tas ah mee ah-mee-gah/ah-mee-goh)

My friend likes you.

Love Languages

Words of affirmation
palabras de afirmación

♥ **Tu bondad nunca deja de sorprenderme.**
(too bon-dahd noon-kah deh-hah deh sor-pren-der-meh)

Your kindness never fails to amaze me.

♥ **Aprecio las cosas que haces por mí.**
(ah-preh-see-oh las koh-sas keh ah-ses por mee)

I appreciate the things you do for me.

♥ **Me encanta cómo me haces reír.**
(meh en-cahn-tah co-moh meh ah-ses reh-eer)

I love how you make me laugh.

♥ **Eres tan sexy que no te puedo resistir.**
(eh-res tahn sexy keh no teh poo-eh-doh reh-sees-teer)

You are so sexy I can't resist you.

Love Languages

Gifting
regalar

♥ **Te hice esta maceta para tus plantas.**
(teh ee-seh es-tah ma-seh-tah pa-rah toos plan-tahs)

I made you this pot for your plants.

♥ **Sé que perdiste tu delantal, así que te compré uno nuevo.**
(seh keh per-dees-teh too deh-lan-tahl, ah-see keh teh com-preh oo-no noo-eh-voh)

I know you lost your apron, so I bought you a new one.

♥ **Aquí tienes $50, gástalo en ti mismo/misma.**
(ah-kee tee-eh-nes $50 gas-ta-loh en tee mees-moh/mees-mah)

Here is $50, spend it on yourself.

♥ **Te compré esta lencería, ¿te gustaría ponértela esta noche?**
(teh com-preh es-tah len-seh-ree-ah, teh goos-tah-ree-ah po-ner-teh-lah es-tah no-che)

I bought you this lingerie, would you like to wear it tonight?

Love Languages

Acts of service
actos de servicio

♥ **Te hice el desayuno.**
(teh ee-seh el des-ah-you-noh)

I made you breakfast.

♥ **¿Necesitas ayuda con la mudanza? Cuenta conmigo.**
(ne-seh-si-tas ah-you-dah con la moo-dan-za coo-en-ta-khon-mee-goh)

Do you need help moving? Count on me.

♥ **Tuviste un día largo, déjame cocinar la cena esta noche.**
(too-bees-teh un dee-ah lar-goh, deh-ha-meh coh-see-nar la seh-nah es-tah no-che)

You've had a long day, let me cook dinner tonight.

♥ **Esta noche yo cuidaré de ti. Solo relájate y disfruta.**

(es-tah no-che yoh coo-ee-da-reh deh tee. so-loh reh-la-hah-teh ee dees-froo-tah)

Tonight I will take care of you. Just sit relax and enjoy.

Love Languages

Quality Time
tiempo de calidad

♥ **Quedémonos en casa y veamos películas.**
(keh-deh-moh-nos en ca-sah ee ve-ah-mos peh-lee-koo-las)

Let's stay home and watch movies.

♥ **Me encanta pasar tiempo contigo.**
(meh en-cahn-tah pa-sar tee-em-poh kohn-tee-goh)

I love spending time with you.

♥ **¿Quieres armar este rompecabezas juntos?**
(kee-eh-rehs ahr-mar es-teh rohm-peh-kah-beh-zas hoon-tohs)

Do you want to work on this puzzle together?

♥ **Quiero que la noche sea nuestra y pasar cada momento en tus brazos.**
(kee-eh-roh keh la no-che seh-ah noo-es-trah ee pa-sar ka-dah moh-men-toh en toos bra-zos)

I want the night to be ours and spend every moment in your arms.

Love Languages

Physical Touch
contacto físico

♥ **caricias**
(cah-ree-see-as)

caresses

♥ **abrazos**
(ah-brah-sos)

hugs

♥ **acurrucarse**
(ah-koo-rue-car-seh)

cuddle/snuggle

♥ **agarrarse de la mano**
(ah-gah-rahr-seh deh la mah-noh)

hand holding

♥ **masajes**
(ma-sa-hehs)

massages

♥ **besos**
(beh-sos)

kisses

♥ **intimidad**
(een-tee-mee-dahd)

intimacy

WAYS TO EXPRESS LOVE

I love you.

Te quiero or **Te amo.**
(teh key-eh-roh) (teh ah-moh)

Remember, 'Te amo' often expresses a deeper feeling, while 'Te quiero' is used more casually.

You are the love of my life.

Eres el amor de mi vida.
(eh-rehs el ah-mohr deh mee vee-dah)

Together forever.

Juntos para siempre.
(hoon-tohs pa-rah see-em-preh)

Our love is eternal.

Nuestro amor es eterno.
(noo-es-troh ah-mohr es eh-ter-noh)

You and I always.

Tú y yo siempre.
(too ee yoh see-em-preh)

I adore you.

Te adoro.
(teh ah-dor-oh)

Affirmations for Self-Love

Soy capaz de alcanzar mis metas.
(soy ka-paz deh al-khan-zar mees meh-tas)

I am capable of achieving my goals.

Soy digno/digna de amor y respeto.
(soy deeg-noh/deeg-nah deh ah-mohr ee res-peh-toh)

I am worthy of love and respect.

Expreso mi verdadero yo con confianza.
(ex-preh-so mee ver-dah-deh-roh yoh khon kon-fee-ahn-zah)

I express my true self with confidence.

Yo merezco felicidad, amor y éxito.
(yoh meh-rhez-coh feh-lee-see-dahd, ah-mohr ee ex-ee-toh)

I deserve happiness, love, and success.

Yo confío en mí para tomar las decisiones correctas.
(yoh kohn-fee-oh en-mee pa-rah toh-mar las deh-see-see-oh-ness co-rec-tahs)

I trust myself to make the right decisions.

Estoy agradecido/agradecida por todo lo que tengo.
(es-toy ah-gra-deh-see-doh/ah-gra-deh-see-dah por toh-doh lo keh ten-goh)

I am grateful for all that I have.

Affirmations for Self-Love

Soy suficiente tal como soy.
(soy sue-fee-see-en-teh tal co-moh soy)

I am enough, just as I am.

Estoy evolucionando hacia mi mejor versión.
(es-toy eh-vo-loo-see-oh-nan-doh ah-see-ah mee meh-hor ver-see-on)

I am evolving into my best version.

Estoy orgulloso/orgullosa de quíen soy.
(es-toy or-goo-yo-soh/or-goo-yo-sah deh kee-ehn soy)

I am proud of who I am.

Me perdono por los errores del pasado.
(meh per-doh-noh por los eh-roh-rhes del pa-sa-doh)

I forgive myself for past mistakes.

Yo acepto los desafíos como oportunidades para crecer.
(yoh ah-sep-toh los deh-sa-fee-ohs co-moh oh-por-too-nee-dah-dehs pa-rah creh-ser)

I accept challenges as opportunities for growth.

Merezco todas las cosas buenas que la vida tiene para ofrecer.
(meh-rez-coh toh-das las koh-sas boo-eh-nas keh la vee-dah tee-eh-neh pa-rah oh-freh-ser)

I am deserving of all the good things life has to offer.

WELLBEING

NOTES:

NOTES:

EL GIMNASIO
(el him-na-see-oh)

The Gym

cardio (kar-dio)	cardio
sentadillas (sen-ta-dee-yas)	squats
saltos de tijera (sal-tos deh tee-heh-rah)	jumping jacks
zancadas (zahn-kah-dahs)	lunges
flexiones (flex-see-oh-nes)	push-ups
correr (koh-rehr)	run
pesas (peh-sas)	dumbbells
cinta de correr (seen-tah deh koh-rehr)	treadmill
elíptica (eh-leep-tee-ka)	elliptical
entrenamiento (en-treh-na-mee-ento)	training
calentamiento (ka-len-ta-mee-ento)	warm-up
enfriamiento (ehn-free-ah-mee-ehn-toh)	cool-down

EL GIMNASIO
(el him-na-see-oh)

The Gym

caminar (kah-mee-nahr)	walk
baile (bah-ee-leh)	dance
yoga (yo-gah)	yoga
entrenamiento cruzado (en-treh-na-mee-ento kroo-sa-doh)	cross-training
series (seh-ree-ehs)	sets
proteína (proh-teh-ee-nah)	protein
pre-entreno (preh ehn-treh-no)	pre-workout
suplementos (sue-pleh-men-tos)	supplements
bebida energética (beh-bee-dah eh-nehr-heh-tee-kah)	energy drink
masa muscular (mah-sah moos-koo-lahr)	muscle mass
estiramiento (es-tee-rah-mee-ento)	stretching

UNA SEMANA DE BIENESTAR MENTAL

A Week of Mental-Wellbeing

lunes

Date un abrazo a ti mismo.
(dah-teh oon ah-brah-soh ah tee mees-moh)

Give yourself a hug.

martes

Sal afuera, mira al cielo y dibuja lo que ves.
(sahl ah-fweh-rah, mee-rah ahl syeh-loh ee dee-boo-hah loh keh behs)

(drawing)

Go outside, look at the sky and draw what you see.

miércoles

Tómate un selfie para recordar este día.
(toh-mah-teh oon sehl-fee pah-rah reh-kor-dahr ehs-teh dee-ah)

Take a selfie to remind you of today.

jueves

Reproduce tu canción favorita y cántala a todo pulmón.
(re-pro-doo-seh too kahn-syohn fah-boh-ree-tah ee kan-ta-la ah toh-doh pool-mon)

_____
(song name)

Play your favorite song and sing it at the top of your lungs.

viernes

Date un cumplido a ti mismo.
(dah-teh oon koom-plee-doh ah tee mis-moh)

_____
(self-compliment)

Give yourself a compliment.

sábado

Estírate durante 5 minutos.
(ehs-tee-rah-teh doo-rahn-teh sin-koh min-oo-tohs)

Stretch for 5 minutes.

domingo

Haz un pequeño acto de amabilidad para alguien.
(ahs oon peh-keh-nyoh ahk-toh deh ah-mah-bee-lee-dahd pah-rah al-gyehn)

Do a small act of kindness for someone.

66

Expressing your mental health concerns

ansiedad — anxiety
(ahn-see-eh-dahd)

depresión — depression
(deh-preh-see-ohn)

ataque de pánico — panic attack
(ah-tah-keh deh pah-nee-koh)

compararse con otros — comparing yourself to others
(kohm-pah-rahr-seh kohn oh-tros)

diálogo interno negativo — negative self–talk
(dee-ah-loh-go in-tehr-no neh-gah-tee-boh)

dieta poco saludable — unhealthy diet
(dee-eh-tah poh-koh sah-loo-dah-bleh)

aislamiento social — social isolation
(ice-lah-mee-en-toh soh-see-ahl)

trastorno de estrés postraumático — post traumatic stress disorder
(trahs-tohr-no deh ehs-tress pohs-trah-oo-mah-tee-koh)

Expressing your mental health concerns

abuso de sustancias
(ah-boo-so deh soos-tahn-see-ahs)

substance abuse

adicción
(ah-deek-see-ohn)

addiction

privación de sueño
(pree-bah-see-ohn deh sue-eh-nyoh)

sleep deprivation

estrés financiero
(ehs-tress fee-nahn-see-eh-roh)

financial stress

culpa crónica
(kool-pah kroh-nee-kah)

chronic guilt

agotamiento
(ah-goh-tah-myehn-toh)

burnout

pensar demasiado
(pehn-sahr deh-mah-see-ah-doh)

overthinking

tiempo excesivo frente a la pantalla
(tee-em-poh ex-seh-see-voh fren-teh ah lah pahn-tah-yah)

excessive screen time

Expressing your mental health concerns

I'm feeling anxious.

Estoy sintiendo ansiedad.
(ehs-toy seen-tee-ehn-doh ahn-see-eh-dahd)

I'm feeling depressed.

Me siento deprimido/deprimida.

(meh see-ehn-toh deh-pree-mee-doh/
deh-pree-mee-dah)

I have trouble sleeping.

Tengo problemas para dormir.
(ten-goh pro-ble-mahs pah-rah door-meer)

I'm starting to have a panic attack.

Estoy empezando a tener un ataque de pánico.

(ehs-toy ehm-peh-san-doh ah teh-nehr
oon ah-tah-keh deh pah-nee-koh)

I have negative thoughts.

Tengo pensamientos negativos.
(ten-go pen-sah-mee-ehn-tohs neh-gah-tee-bohs)

I need help.

Necesito ayuda.

(neh-seh-see-toh ah-yoo-dah)

Taking Care of Your Mental Health

DESCANSO DE REDES SOCIALES → SOCIAL MEDIA BREAK
(des-kahn-soh deh reh-dehs soh-see-ah-lehs)

MEDITACIÓN → MEDITATION
(meh-dee-tah-see-on)

TERAPIA – THERAPY
(teh-rah-pee-ah)

ORAR – PRAY
(oh-rahr)

HÁBITOS DE ALIMENTACIÓN SALUDABLE → HEALTHY EATING HABITS
(ah-bee-tohs deh ah-lee-mehn-tah-see-ohn sah-loo-dah-bleh)

DORMIR BIEN – SLEEP WELL
(door-meer bee-ehn)

REÍR – LAUGH
(reh-eer)

Taking Care of Your Mental Health

PASAR TIEMPO EN LA NATURALEZA
(pah-sahr tee-ehm-poh ehn lah nah-too-rah-leh-sah)
→ SPENDING TIME IN NATURE

ESTABLECER LÍMITES ↔ SETTING BOUNDARIES
(ehs-tah-bleh-sehr lee-mee-tehs)

↪ **BUSCAR AYUDA**
(boos-kahr ah-yoo-dah)
SEEK HELP

ESCRIBIR EN UN DIARIO
(ehs-kree-bihr ehn oon dee-ah-ree-oh)
JOURNALING ↩

PENSAMIENTOS POSITIVOS SOBRE UNO MISMO
(pehn-sah-mee-ehn-tohs poh-see-tee-bohs soh-breh oo-noh mees-moh)
↪ POSITIVE SELF-TALK

Recordatorio.

Un poco de progreso cada día suma grandes resultados.

Reminder.

A little progress every day adds up to great results.

HOME AND FAMILY

NOTES:

NOTES:

CASA - HOME
(cah-sah)

dirección — address
(dee-rehk-see-ohn)

depa/departamento — apartment
(deh-pah/deh-pahr-tah-men-toh)

condominio — condo/condominium
(kohn-doh-mee-nee-oh)

vecindario — neighborhood
(veh-seen-dah-ree-oh)

mansión — mansion
(mahn-see-ohn)

refugio — shelter
(reh-foo-hee-oh)

hogar de ancianos — nursing home
(oh-gahr deh ahn-see-ah-nohs)

HABITACIONES - ROOMS
(ah-bee-tah-see-ohn-nehs)

sótano (soh-tah-noh)	basement
cochera/garaje (koh-cheh-rah/gah-rah-heh)	garage
cocina (koh-see-nah)	kitchen
comedor (koh-meh-dohr)	dining room
sala (sah-lah)	living room
baño (bah-nyoh)	bathroom
cuarto (kwahr-toh)	room
atico (ah-tee-koh)	attic
oficina (oh-fee-see-nah)	office
sala de huéspedes (sah-lah deh wes-peh-des)	guest room
balcón (bahl-kohn)	balcony
cuarto de lavado (kwahr-toh deh lah-bah-doh)	laundry room

EN LA CASA - AROUND THE HOUSE
(ehn la cah-sah)

cama (kah-mah) — bed

tocador (toh-kah-dohr) — dresser

espejo (ehs-peh-hoh) — mirror

escritorio (ehs-kree-toh-ree-oh) — desk

sofá (soh-fah) — couch

television (teh-leh-bee-see-ohn) — television

mesa de centro (meh-sah deh sehn-troh) — coffee table

mesa (meh-sah) — table

silla (see-yah) — chair

trastes (trahs-tes) — dishes

alfombra (ahl-fohm-brah) — carpet/rug

lavabo (lah-vah-boh) — sink

inodoro (ee-noh-doh-roh) — toilet

bañera (bah-nyeh-rah) — bathtub

caja de seguridad (kah-hah deh seh-goo-ree-dahd) — safebox

retrato (reh-trah-toh) — portrait

lámpara (lahm-pah-rah) — lamp

escaleras (ehs-kah-leh-rahs) — stairs

pasillo (pah-see-yoh) — hallway

puerta (pooh-ehr-tah) — door

timbre (teem-breh) — doorbell

ventana (behn-tah-nah) — window

pared (pah-rehd) — wall

chimenea (chee-meh-neh-ah) — chimney

toma de corriente (toh-mah deh koh-ree-ehn-teh) — outlet

ELECTRODOMÉSTICOS - HOUSEHOLD APPLIANCES
(eh-lehk-tro-doh-mehs-tee-kohs)

refrigerador (reh-free-heh-rah-dohr)	refrigerator
congelador (khon-hell-ah-dohr)	freezer
estufa (es-too-fah)	stove
microondas (mee-crow-on-dahs)	microwave
lavaplatos (lah-bah-plah-tohs)	dishwasher
lavadora (lah-bah-doh-rah)	washing machine
secadora (seh-kah-doh-rah)	dryer
licuadora (lee-kwah-doh-rah)	blender
tostador (tohs-tah-dohr)	toaster
cafetera (kah-feh-teh-rah)	coffee maker
tetera (teh-teh-rah)	kettle
horno (or-noh)	oven
batidora (bah-tee-doh-rah)	mixer
parrilla eléctrica (pah-ree-yah eh-lehk-tree-kah)	electric grill

¿Por qué la licuadora regresó con su ex?

-Porque tenía emociones revueltas.

Why did the blender get back with its ex?
-Because it had mixed emotions.

AL AIRE LIBRE - OUTDOORS
(ahl ah-ee-reh lee-breh)

entrada de coche (en-trah-dah deh koh-cheh)	driveway
banqueta (bahn-keh-tah)	sidewalk
buzón (boo-zohn)	mailbox
patio trasero (pah-tee-oh trah-seh-roh)	backyard
paneles solares (pah-neh-lehs soh-lah-rehs)	solar panels
árboles (ahr-boh-les)	trees

Match the picture to the correct Spanish word.

trampolín
(tram-poh-lean)

jardín
(har-deen)

cerca
(sehr-kah)

parrilla
(pah-ree-yah)

piscina/alberca
(pee-see-nah/al-behr-kah)

QUEHACERES - CHORES
(keh-ah-seh-rehs)

KITCHEN

lavar los trastes — wash the dishes
(lah-bahr los trahs-tehs)

barrer — sweep
(bah-rehr)

trapear — mop
(trah-peh-ahr)

limpiar la encimera — wipe down countertop
(leem-pee-ahr la ehn-cee-meh-rah)

sacar la basura — take out the trash
(sah-kahr la bah-sue-rah)

limpiar el refrigerador — clean out the refrigerator
(leem-pee-ahr el reh-free-heh-rah-dohr)

organizar la despensa — organize the pantry
(or-gah-nee-zhar la dehs-pen-sah)

BEDROOM

tender la cama — make bed
(ten-dher la kah-mah)

aspirar la alfombra — vacuum carpet
(ahs-pee-rahr la ahl-foam-brah)

sacudir las superficies — dusting surfaces
(sah-koo-dihr lahs super-fee-see-ehs)

vaciar los botes de basura — empty out trash bins
(bah-see-ahr los boh-tehs de bah-sue-rah)

ordenar — declutter
(ohr-deh-nahr)

BATHROOM

fregar el inodoro — scrub toilet
(freh-gahr el ee-noh-dohr-oh)

limpiar el lavabo — clean sink
(leem-pee-ahr el lah-bah-boh)

desinfectar — disinfect
(deh-seen-fehk-tar)

limpiar el espejo — wipe down mirror
(leem-pee-ahr el ehs-peh-ho)

cambiar las toallas — replace towels
(kham-bee-ahr las toh-ah-yas)

LAUNDRY

lavar la ropa — laundry
(lah-bar la roh-pah)

secar la ropa — dry the clothes
(seh-car la roh-pah)

doblar la ropa — fold the clothes
(doh-blar la roh-pah)

planchar la ropa — iron the clothes
(plahn-char la roh-pah)

la tintoreria — dry cleaning
(la teen-toh-reh-ree-ah)

OUTSIDE CHORES

cortar el césped   mow the lawn
(kohr-tar el ses-ped)

rastrillar las hojas   rake the leaves
(ras-tree-yar las oh-has)

desyerbar   weeding
(des-yer-bar)

regar las plantas/el césped   water the plants/grass
(reh-gar las plahn-tahs/el ses-ped)

palear la nieve   shovel the snow
(pah-leh-ahr la nee-eh-veh)

organizar el garaje   organize the garage
(or-gah-nee-zahr el gah-rah-heh)

VEHICLE MAINTENANCE

lavar el carro   wash the car
(lah-bahr el kah-roh)

aspirar el carro   vacuum the car
(ahs-pee-rahr el kah-roh)

cambio de aceite   oil change
(kam-bee-oh de ah-say-teh)

llenar el tanque de gasolina   fill-up the gas tank
(yeh-nar el tan-keh de gas-oh-lee-nah)

CLEANING SUPPLIES

plumero
(ploo-meh-roh)

duster

guantes de goma
(gwan-tehs de go-mah)

rubber gloves

toallas húmedas
(toh-ah-yas oo-meh-dahs)

wet wipes

ambientador
(ahm-bee-en-tah-dohr)

air freshner

vela
(veh-lah)

candle

aspiradora
(ahs-pee-rah-doh-rah)

vacuum

Write the correct number next to the Spanish word.

1.
2.
3.
4.
5.
6.

_____ **escoba**
(ehs-co-bah)

_____ **trapeador**
(tra-peh-ah-dohr)

_____ **esponja**
(es-pon-hah)

_____ **cubeta**
(coo-beh-tah)

_____ **recogedor**
(reh-koh-heh-dohr)

_____ **jabón**
(ha-bohn)

CLEANING
CHECKLIST

DIARIO - DAILY

- ☐ Tender la cama
- ☐ Lavar los trastes
- ☐ Limpiar la encimera
- ☐ Desinfectar el baño

WEEKLY - SEMANAL

- ☐ Lavar la ropa
- ☐ Aspirar la alfombra
- ☐ Sacudir las superficies
- ☐ Sacar la basura
- ☐ Limpiar el espejo
- ☐ Trapear

MONTHLY - MENSUAL

- ☐ Ordenar
- ☐ Limpiar el refrigerador
- ☐ Organizar la despensa
- ☐ Organizar el garaje

FAMILIA
FAMILY

padres {
(pah-dress)
parents

- **madre** (mah-dreh) — mother
- **mamá** (mah-mah) — mom
- **ma/amá** (mah/ah-mah) — momma
- **mami** (mah-mee) — mommy
- **madrastra** (mah-drah-strah) — stepmom
- **padre** (pah-dreh) — father
- **papá** (pah-pah) — dad
- **pa/apá** (pah/ah-pah) — dad
- **papi** (pah-pee) — daddy
- **padrastro** (pah-drah-stroh) — stepdad

maternal – maternal (mah-ter-nahl)

paternal – paternal (pah-ter-nahl)

FAMILIA
FAMILY

hermanos
(ehr-mah-nohs)

siblings

- **hermana** (ehr-mah-nah) — sister
- **carnala** (kahr-nah-lah) — sister/sis
- **hermanastra** (ehr-mah-nahs-trah) — stepsister
- **media hermana** (meh-dee-ah ehr-mah-nah) — half-sister
- **hermano** (ehr-mah-noh) — brother
- **carnal** (kahr-nahl) — brother/bro
- **hermanastro** (ehr-mah-nahs-troh) — stepbrother
- **medio hermano** (meh-dee-oh ehr-mah-noh) — half-brother

niños/niñas
(nee-nyohs/nee-nyahs)
children
- **hija** (ee-hah) — daughter
- **hijastra** (ee-hah-strah) — stepdaughter
- **hijo** (ee-hoh) — son
- **hijastro** (ee-hah-stroh) — stepson

abuelos
(ah-boo-eh-lohs)
grandparents
- **abuela** (ah-boo-eh-lah) — grandmother
- **abuelita** (ah-boo-eh-lee-tah) — grandmother
- **abuelo** (ah-boo-eh-loh) — grandfather
- **abuelito** (ah-boo-eh-lee-toh) — grandfather

nietos
(nee-eh-tohs)
grandchildren
- **nieta** (nee-eh-tah) — granddaughter
- **nieto** (nee-eh-toh) — grandson

tia (tee-ah) — aunt

tio (tee-oh) — uncle

prima (pree-mah) — female cousin

primo (pree-moh) — male cousin

sobrina (soh-bree-nah) — niece

sobrino (soh-bree-noh) — nephew

parientes politicos
(pah-ree-ehn-tes poh-lee-tee-kohs)

in-laws

- **suegra** (sue-eh-grah) — mother-in-law
- **suegro** (sue-eh-groh) — father-in-law
- **cuñada** (koo-nyah-dah) — sister-in-law
- **cuñado** (koo-nyah-doh) — bother-in-law
- **nuera** (noo-eh-rah) — daughter-in-law
- **nuero** (noo-eh-roh) — son-in-law

Remember: In situations where a group contains masculine and feminine nouns, use the masculine plural form to refer to the entire group. For example, 'mis primos' can indicate a group of male cousins or a mix of male and female cousins.

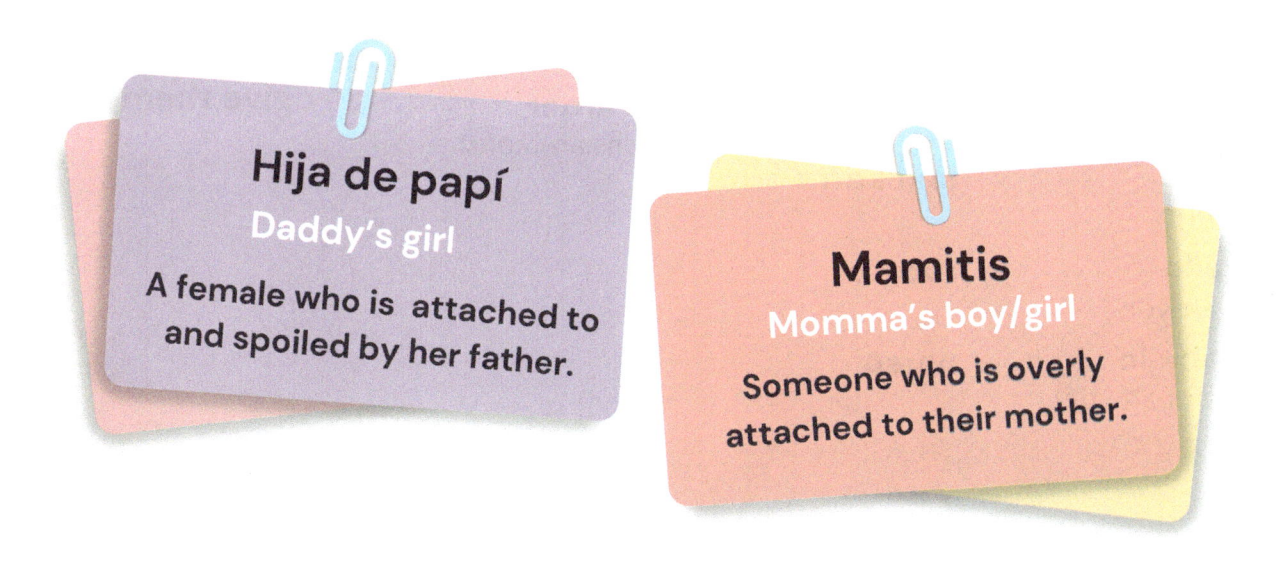

Hija de papí
Daddy's girl

A female who is attached to and spoiled by her father.

Mamitis
Momma's boy/girl

Someone who is overly attached to their mother.

MASCOTAS
PETS

perro — dog
(peh-roh)

gato — cat
(gah-toh)

conejo — rabbit
(koh-neh-hoh)

pescado/pez — fish
(pez-kah-doh/pez)

hámster — hamster
(hamster)

cobayo — guinea pig
(koh-bah-yoh)

serpiente — snake
(sehr-pee-ehn-teh)

tortuga — turtle
(tohr-too-gah)

pájaro — bird
(pah-hah-roh)

loro — parrot
(loh-roh)

lagarto — lizard
(lah-gahr-toh)

pollo — chicken
(poh-yoh)

gallo — rooster
(gah-yoh)

caballo — horse
(kah-bah-yoh)

recoger la caca — pick-up the poop
(reh-koh-her la kah-kah)

limpiar la jaula — clean the cage
(leem-pee-ahr la hah-oo-lah)

arena para gatos — cat litter
(ah-reh-nah pah-rah gah-tohs)

caminar al perro — dog walk
(kah-mee-nahr ahl peh-rroh)

parque de perros — dog park
(pahr-keh de peh-rrohs)

el aseo — grooming
(el ah-seh-oh)

dar de comer — feed
(dahr deh koh-mehr)

entrenar — train
(ehn-treh-nahr)

tiempo para jugar — playtime
(tee-ehm-poh pah-rah hoo-gahr)

darles amor — give them love
(dahr-lehs ah-mohr)

GRWM

NOTES:

NOTES:

GRWM
Get Ready With Me

CUIDADO DE LA PIEL - SKIN CARE
(kwee-dah-doh deh lah pee-ehl)

limpiador facial — facial cleanser
(leem-pee-ah-dor fah-see-ahl)

exfoliante — exfoliant
(ex-foh-lee-ahn-teh)

tonificador — toner
(toh-nee-fee-kah-door)

suero facial — facial serum
(sue-eh-roh fah-see-ahl)

crema hidratante — moisturizer
(kreh-mah ee-drah-tahn-teh)

crema para los ojos — eye cream
(kreh-mah pah-rah los oh-hos)

protector solar — sunscreen
(proh-tek-tohr so-lahr)

HIGIENE - HYGIENE
(ee-hee-eh-neh)

bañarse — to shower
(bah-nyahr-seh)

champú — shampoo
(cham-poo)

acondicionador — conditioner
(ah-kohn-dee-see-oh-nah-dor)

gel de baño — body wash
(hel deh bah-nyo)

esponja de baño — shower sponge
(ehs-pohn-ha deh bah-nyo)

rasurar/afeitar — shave
(rah-sue-rar/ah-fay-tar)

desodorante — deodorant
(deh-soh-doh-rahn-teh)

cepillar los dientes — brush your teeth
(seh-pee-yar lohs dyehn-tehs)

cepillo de dientes — toothbrush
(seh-pee-yoh deh dyehn-tehs)

pasta de dientes — toothpaste
(pahs-tah deh dyehn-tehs)

enjuague bucal — mouthwash
(ehn-who-ah-geh boo-kahl)

hilo dental — dental floss
(ee-loh den-tahl)

GRWM TO GO TO SCHOOL
Get Ready With Me

PERSONAL ESCOLAR - SCHOOL STAFF
(pehr-soh-nahl ehs-koh-lahr)

maestro/maestra (mah-ehs-tro/mah-ehs-tra)	teacher
orientador/orientadora (oh-ree-en-ta-dohr/oh-ree-en-ta-do-rah)	counselor
director/directora (dee-rec-tor/dee-rec-toh-rah)	principal
enfermero/enfermera (ehn-fer-meh-roh/ehn-fer-meh-rah)	nurse
conserje (kohn-sehr-heh)	janitor
chofer de autobús (cho-fehr deh ow-toh-boos)	bus driver
vigilante (bee-hee-lahn-teh)	security guard

UTILES ESCOLARES - SCHOOL SUPPLIES
(oo-tee-les es-koh-lah-rehs)

mochila (moh-chee-lah)	backpack	**papel** (pah-pel)	paper
libro (lee-broh)	book	**cinta adhesiva** (seen-tah ah-de-see-vah)	tape
lápiz (lah-peez)	pencil	**sacapuntas** (sah-kah-poon-tahs)	sharpener
pluma (ploo-mah)	pen	**grapadora** (grah-pah-doh-rah)	stapler
cuaderno (kwah-dehr-noh)	notebook	**carpeta** (kahr-peh-tah)	binder
marcadores (mahr-kah-doh-rehs)	markers	**calculadora** (kahl-koo-lah-doh-rah)	calculator
computadora portátil (kohm-poo-tah-doh-rah por-tah-teel)	laptop	**planificador** (plah-nee-fee-kah-dohr)	planner

GRWM TO GO TO THE GYM
Get Ready With Me

tenis (teh-nees) — sneakers

shorts (shorts) — shorts

ropa deportiva (roh-pah deh-por-tee-vah) — sports clothes

faja (fah-hah) — waist trainer

audífonos (ow-dee-foh-nos) — headphones

guantes de gimnasio (gwahn-tes deh him-nah-see-oh) — gym gloves

botella de agua (boh-teh-yah deh ah-gwah) — water bottle

toalla (toh-ah-yah) — towel

GRWM TO GO TO WORK
Get Ready With Me

casco de seguridad (kaz-ko deh seh-goo-ree-dahd) — safety hat

chaleco de seguridad (cha-leh-ko deh seh-goo-ree-dahd) — safety vest

uniforme (oo-nee-for-meh) — uniform

uniforme médico (oo-nee-for-meh meh-dee-koh) — scrubs

traje (trah-heh) — suit

maleta (mah-leh-tah) — suitcase

ropa de negocios informal (roh-pah deh neh-go-see-ohs een-for-mahl) — business casual

gafete (gah-feh-teh) — badge

herramientas (eh-rra-mee-en-tas) — tools

fichar entrada (fee-char en-trah-dah) — clock-in

fichar salida (fee-char sah-lee-dah) — clock-out

GRWM FOR A NIGHT OUT
Get Ready With Me

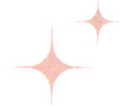

● MAQUILLAJE - MAKEUP
(mah-kee-yah-heh)

prebase (preh-bah-seh)	primer
corrector (coh-rehk-tohr)	concealer
base de maquillaje (bah-seh deh mah-kee-yah-heh)	foundation
bronceador (brohn-seh-ah-dohr)	bronzer
rubor (roo-bohr)	blush
lápiz de cejas (lah-peez deh seh-hahs)	brow pencil
sombra de ojos (sohm-brah deh oh-hos)	eyeshadow
rimel (ree-mehl)	mascara
pestañas (pez-tah-nyahs)	lashes
fijador en spray (fee-hah-dohr en ehs-pray)	setting spray
lápiz labial (lah-peez lah-bee-ahl)	lip pencil
brillo labial (bree-yoh lah-bee-ahl)	lipgloss
labial (lah-bee-ahl)	lipstick
brocha de maquillaje (broh-chah deh mah-kee-yah-heh)	makeup brush

perfume de hombre
(pehr-foo-meh deh ohm-breh)

cologne

perfume
(pehr-foo-meh)

perfume

● JOYERÍA - JEWERLY
(ho-yeh-ree-ah)

aretes (ah-reh-tes)	earrings
pulsera (pool-seh-rah)	bracelet
collar (koh-yahr)	necklace
anillo (ah-nee-yo)	ring
reloj (reh-loH)	watch

zapatos de vestir
(sah-pah-tos deh behs-teer)
dress shoes

botas
(boh-tahs)
boots

tacones altos
(tah-koh-nes ahl-tos)
high heels

sandalias
(sahn-dah-lee-ahs)
sandals

SHOPPING

NOTES:

NOTES:

Getting Help at The Store

Disculpa, ¿me puedes ayudar?   Excuse me, can you help me?
(deez-kool-pah, meh poo-eh-dehs ah-yoo-dar)

¿Me puedes ayudar a encontrar...?   Can you help me find ...?
(meh poo-eh-dehs ah-yoo-dar ah en-kohn-trar)

¿Tú trabajas aquí?   Do you work here?
(too trah-bah-hahs ah-kee)

¿Cuánto cuesta?   How much is it?
(koo-ahn-toh koo-ehs-tah)

¿Cuál es el total?   What is the total?
(koo-ahl es el toh-tahl)

¿Me puedes dar un recibo de regalo?   Can you give me a gift receipt?
(meh poo-eh-dehs dar un reh-see-boh de reh-gah-loh)

¿Me puedo probar esto?   Can I try this on?
(meh poo-eh-doh proh-bar ehs-toh)

¿Tienen probadores?   Do you have dressing rooms?
(tee-eh-nehn proh-bah-doh-rehs)

¿Dónde están los probadores?   Where are the dressing rooms?
(dohn-deh ehs-tahn los proh-bah-doh-rehs)

Getting Help at The Store

¿Cómo me queda esto?
(koh-moh me keh-dah ehs-toh)

How does this fit me?

¿Cómo se me ve?
(koh-moh se meh veh)

How does this look on me?

¿Hay algunas ofertas?
(ay ahl-goo-nahs oh-fer-tahs)

Are there any offers/deals?

¿Ofrecen garantía?
(oh-freh-zen gah-rahn-tee-ah)

Do you offer warranty?

¿Cuál es el horario de la tienda?
(koo-ahl es el orah-ree-oh de la tee-ehn-dah)

What are your store hours?

¿Qué producto recomiendas?
(keh proh-dook-toh reh-koh-mee-ehn-das)

What product do you recommend?

¿Cuál es tu política de devoluciones?
(koo-ahl es too poh-lee-tee-kah de deh-boh-loo-see-oh-nehs)

What is your return policy?

¿Puedo hablar con el gerente?
(poo-eh-doh ah-blahr kohn el heh-ren-teh)

Can I speak to the manager?

Getting Help at The Store

¿Tienes esto en diferente <u>color</u>? Do you have this in a different <u>color</u>?
(tee-eh-nehs ehs-toh en dee-feh-rehn-teh koh-lohr)

<u>estilo</u> — style
(ehs-tee-loh)

<u>talla</u> — size
(tah-yah)

Estoy buscando algo <u>elegante</u>. I'm looking for something <u>elegant</u>.
(ehs-toy boos-kahn-doh ahl-goh ehl-eh-gahn-teh)

<u>cómodo</u> — comfortable
(koh-moh-doh)

<u>casual</u> — casual
(kah-sue-ahl)

<u>profesional</u> — professional
(proh-feh-see-oh-nahl)

¿Puedo pagar con <u>tarjeta de crédito</u>? Can I pay with a <u>credit card</u>?
(pooh-eh-doh pah-gahr kohn tahr-heh-tah de kreh-dee-toh)

<u>tarjeta de débito</u> — debit card
(tahr-heh-tah de deh-bee-toh)

<u>efectivo</u> — cash
(eh-fehk-tee-voh)

Getting Help at The Store

Estoy buscando algo similar pero más barato.
(ehs-toy boos-kahn-doh ahl-goh see-mee-lahr peh-roh mahs bah-rah-toh)

I'm looking for something similar but cheaper in price.

Prefiero un color más oscuro/claro.
(preh-fee-eh-roh oon koh-lohr mahs ohs-koo-roh/klah-roh)

I prefer a darker/lighter color.

Me gustaría cambiar este vestido.
(meh goos-tah-ree-ah kahm-bee-ahr ehs-teh ves-tee-doh)

I would like to exchange this dress.

Quiero comprar estos chocolates.
(kee-eh-roh kohm-prahr ehs-tohs choh-koh-lah-tehs)

I want to buy these chocolates.

Necesito devolver estos pantalones.
(neh-seh-see-toh deh-vohl-ver ehs-tos pahn-tah-loh-ness)

I need to return these pants.

Getting Help at The Store

Esto es exactamente lo que buscaba.
(ehs-toh es exak-tah-men-teh lo keh boos-kah-bah)

This is exactly what I was looking for.

Gracias por tu ayuda.
(grah-see-ahs por too ah-yoo-dah)

Thanks for your help.

Cambié de opinión sobre este artículo.
(kahm-bee-eh de oh-pee-nee-on soh-breh es-teh ar-tee-koo-loh)

I changed my mind about this item.

Me gustaría saber más sobre este perfume.
(meh goos-tah-ree-ah sa-behr mas soh-breh es-teh per-foo-meh)

I would like to know more about this perfume.

Getting Help at The Store

Se ve muy ocupado hoy.
(seh veh mooy oh-koo-pah-doh oh-ee)

It looks very busy today.

Este producto está vencido.
(es-teh pro-dook-toh es-tah ven-see-doh)

This product is expired.

Estoy molesto/molesta con la calidad de este producto.
(es-toy moh-les-toh/moh-les-tah khon la kah-lee-dahd deh es-teh pro-dook-toh)

I'm upset with the quality of this product.

Estoy contento/contenta con el servicio al cliente.
(es-toy kohn-ten-toh/kohn-ten-tah kohn el ser-vee-see-oh al clee-en-teh)

I'm happy with the customer service.

No estaba al tanto de los cargos adicionales.
(no es-tah-bah al tahn-toh de los car-gohs ah-dee-see-oh-nah-lehs)

I was not aware of the extra charges.

Gift shopping for an adult

ropa
(roh-pah)
clothes

accesorios
(awk-seh-soh-ree-ohs)
accessories

cosméticos
(kohs-meh-tee-kohs)
cosmetics

electrónicos
(eh-lehk-troh-nee-kohs)
electronics

vino
(vee-noh)
wine

tarjeta de regalo
(tahr-heh-tah deh reh-gah-loh)
gift card

herramientas
(eh-rah-mee-ehn-tahs)
tools

Gift shopping for a kid

juguetes
(hoo-geh-tehs)
toys

muñecas
(moo-nye-kahs)
dolls

videojuegos
(vee-deh-oh-who-eh-gohs)
video games

peluches
(peh-loo-chess)
stuffed animals

juegos de mesa
(hoo-eh-gohs de meh-sah)
board games

artículos deportivos
(ar-tee-koo-lohs deh-por-tee-voh)
sports gear

bicicleta/bici
(bee-see-kleh-tah/bee-see)
bicycle/bike

Shopping for a party

invitaciones (een-vee-tah-see-oh-nehs)	invitations
globos (gloh-bohs)	ballons
mantel (mahn-tehl)	tablecloth
banderín (bahn-deh-reen)	banner
confeti (kohn-feh-tee)	confetti
velas de cumpleaños (veh-lahs de koom-pleh-ah-nyohs)	birthday candles
pastel/pastelitos (pahs-tehl/pahs-teh-lee-tohs)	cake/cupcakes
bocadillos (boh-kah-dee-yohs)	snacks
bebidas (beh-bee-dahs)	drinks
vasos de plástico/cubiertos (bah-sohs de plahs-tee-koh/koo-bee-ehr-tohs)	plastic cups/utensils

♦ **¿Dónde puedo encontrar las bolsas de regalo?**
(don-deh poo-eh-doh en-kohn-trar las bol-sahs de reh-gah-loh)
Where can I find the gift bags?

♦ **¿Qué tipo de decoraciones tienen para una fiesta?**
(keh tee-poh de de-co-rah-see-oh-ness tee-eh-nen pa-rah oona fee-es-tah)
What kind of party decorations do you have?

GROCERY SHOPPING
el mandado

las frutas y verduras
(las froo-tahs ee ver-doo-rahs)

fruits and vegetables

las carnes
(las kar-nehs)

meats

los lácteos
(los lack-teh-ohs)

dairy

la charcutería
(la char-coo-teh-ree-ah)

deli

los mariscos
(los ma-rees-kohs)

seafood

la panadería
(la pa-na-deh-ree-ah)

bakery

los alimentos congelados
(los ali-men-tohs kohn-heh-la-dohs)

frozen food

los alimentos orgánicos
(los ali-men-tohs or-ga-nee-kohs)

organic food

los granos/nueces
(los grah-nohs/noo-eh-ses)

grains/nuts

la comida enlatada
(la koh-mee-dah en-la-tah-dah)

canned food

las bebidas
(las beh-bee-dahs)

beverages

Grocery List

Use this grocery list to practice your Spanish in the real world.

frutas y verduras

- [ ] _____
- [ ] _____
- [ ] _____
- [ ] _____
- [ ] _____
- [ ] _____

carnes y charcutería

- [ ] _____
- [ ] _____
- [ ] _____
- [ ] _____
- [ ] _____
- [ ] _____

lácteos

- [ ] _____
- [ ] _____
- [ ] _____
- [ ] _____
- [ ] _____
- [ ] _____

alimentos congelados

- [ ] _____
- [ ] _____
- [ ] _____
- [ ] _____
- [ ] _____
- [ ] _____

TEST YOUR UNDERSTANDING
Lesson 8 Shopping

1. When you say, "¿Me puedes dar un recibo de regalo?" you are asking for a gift receipt.

    A. True

    B. False

2. If a product was expired, you would say "Esto es exactamente lo que buscaba."

    A. True

    B. False

3. You can find mariscos at la panaderia.

    A. True

    B. False

4. If you see globos, velas de cumpleaños, y un pastel, you are at a birthday party.

    A. True

    B. False

Answer Key

Test your understanding. Lesson 1 Grammar

1. **a**
2. **c**
3. **b**
4. **b**

Match the picture to the correct Spanish word. Lesson 6 Home and Family

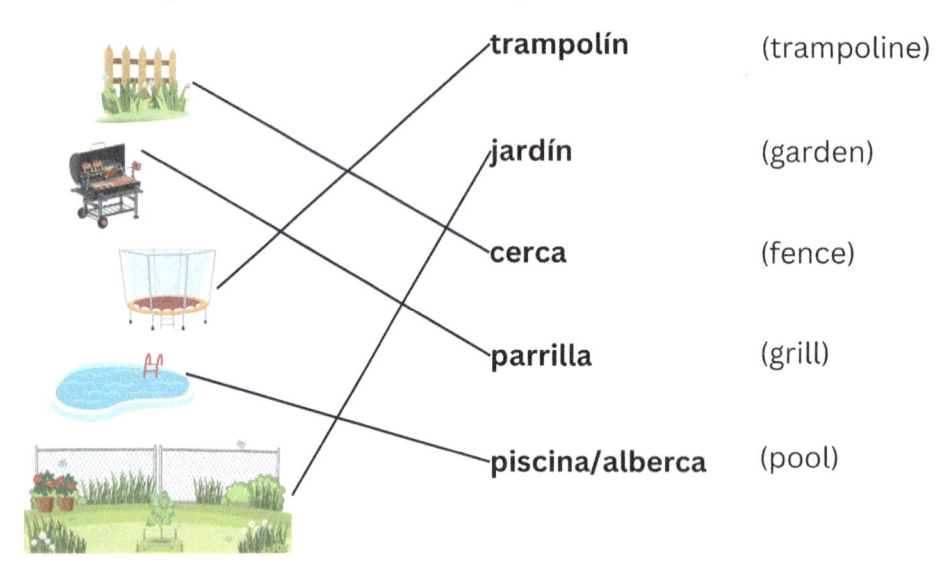

trampolín (trampoline)

jardín (garden)

cerca (fence)

parrilla (grill)

piscina/alberca (pool)

Match the correct number next to the Spanish word. Lesson 6 Home and Family

4. **escoba** (broom)
1. **trapeador** (mop)
5. **esponja** (sponge)
2. **cubeta** (bucket)
3. **recojedor** (dustpan)
6. **jabón** (soap)

Test your understanding. Lesson 8 Shopping

1. **a**
2. **b**
3. **b**
4. **a**

MY NOTES

MY NOTES

MY NOTES

Made in United States
North Haven, CT
31 March 2025